FOR ORGANS, PIANOS & ELECTRONIC KEYBOARDS

E·Z PLAY® TODAY

81

MUSIC FROM MINECRAFT

T0071619

ISBN 978-1-70517-604-7

HAL•LEONARD®

Visit Hal Leonard Online at
**www.halleonard.com**

World headquarters, contact:
**Hal Leonard**
7777 West Bluemound Road
Milwaukee, WI 53213
Email: info@halleonard.com

In Europe, contact:
**Hal Leonard Europe Limited**
1 Red Place
London, W1K 6PL
Email: info@halleonardeurope.com

In Australia, contact:
**Hal Leonard Australia Pty. Ltd.**
4 Lentara Court
Cheltenham, Victoria, 3192 Australia
Email: info@halleonard.com.au

# Registration Guide

- Match the Registration number on the song to the corresponding numbered category below. Select and activate an instrumental sound available on your instrument.

- Choose an automatic rhythm appropriate to the mood and style of the song. (Consult your Owner's Guide for proper operation of automatic rhythm features.)

- Adjust the tempo and volume controls to comfortable settings.

## Registration

| | | |
|---|---|---|
| 1 | Mellow | Flutes, Clarinet, Oboe, Flugel Horn, Trombone, French Horn, Organ Flutes |
| 2 | Ensemble | Brass Section, Sax Section, Wind Ensemble, Full Organ, Theater Organ |
| 3 | Strings | Violin, Viola, Cello, Fiddle, String Ensemble, Pizzicato, Organ Strings |
| 4 | Guitars | Acoustic/Electric Guitars, Banjo, Mandolin, Dulcimer, Ukulele, Hawaiian Guitar |
| 5 | Mallets | Vibraphone, Marimba, Xylophone, Steel Drums, Bells, Celesta, Chimes |
| 6 | Liturgical | Pipe Organ, Hand Bells, Vocal Ensemble, Choir, Organ Flutes |
| 7 | Bright | Saxophones, Trumpet, Mute Trumpet, Synth Leads, Jazz/Gospel Organs |
| 8 | Piano | Piano, Electric Piano, Honky Tonk Piano, Harpsichord, Clavi |
| 9 | Novelty | Melodic Percussion, Wah Trumpet, Synth, Whistle, Kazoo, Perc. Organ |
| 10 | Bellows | Accordion, French Accordion, Mussette, Harmonica, Pump Organ, Bagpipes |

# Alpha
## from MINECRAFT: VOLUME BETA

By Daniel Rosenfeld

Registration 8
Rhythm: None

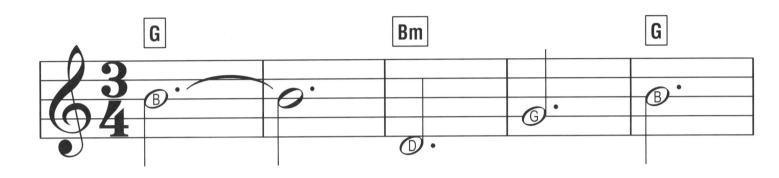

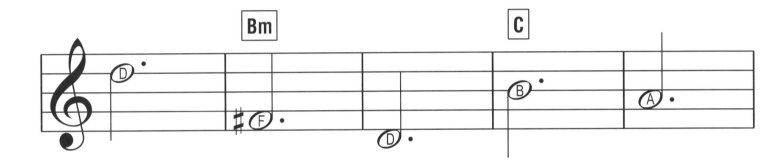

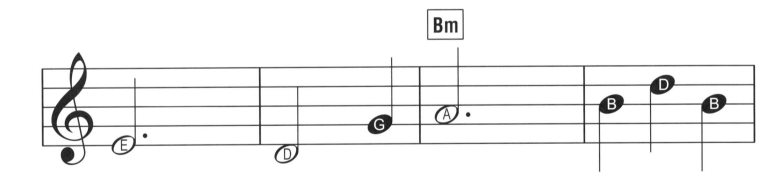

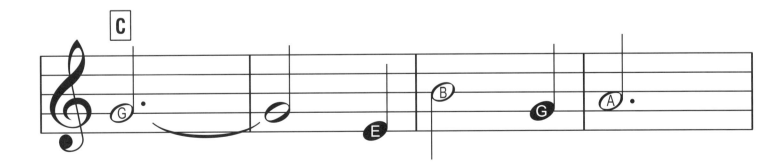

5

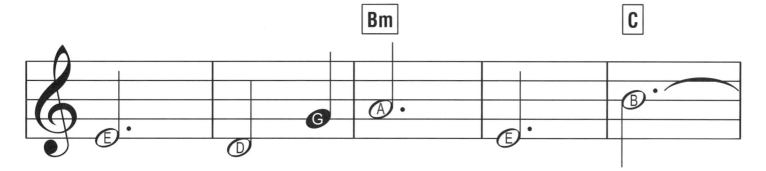

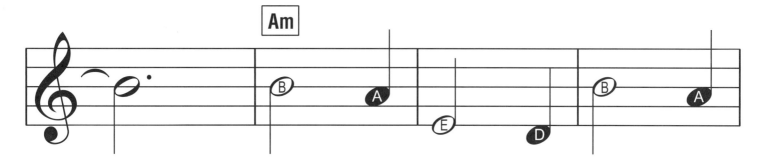

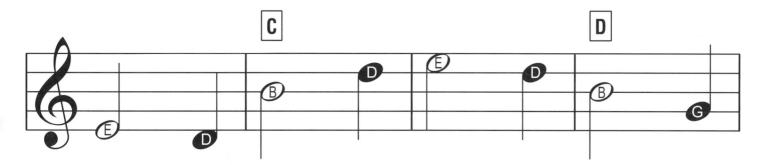

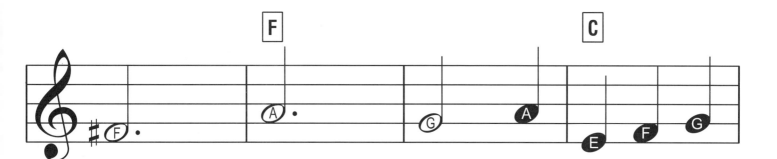

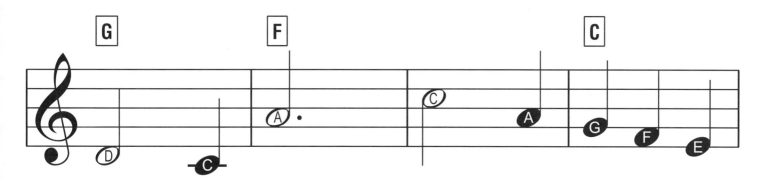

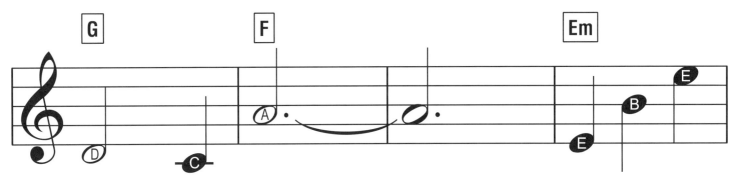

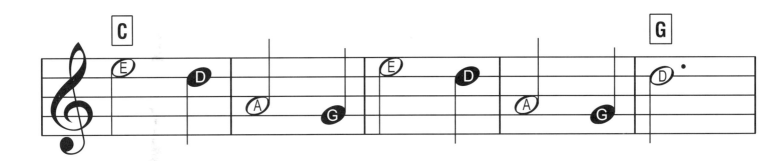

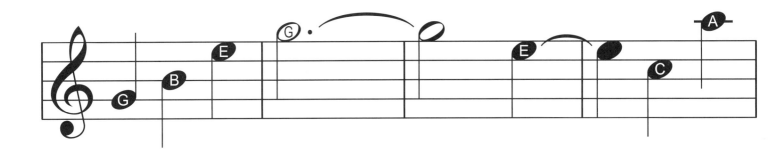

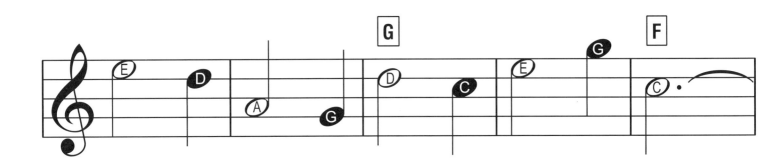

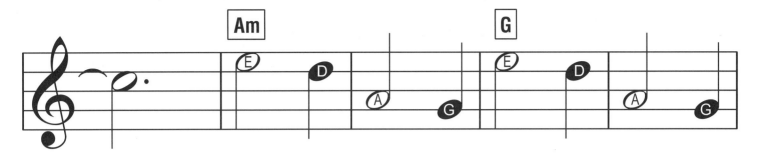

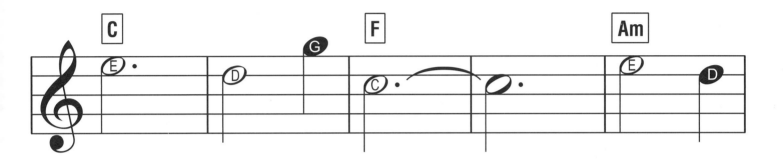

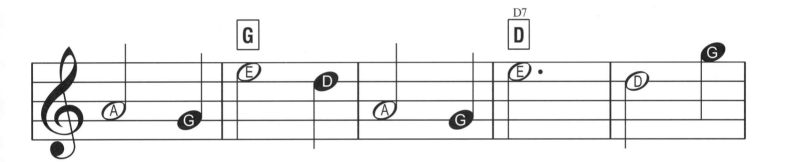

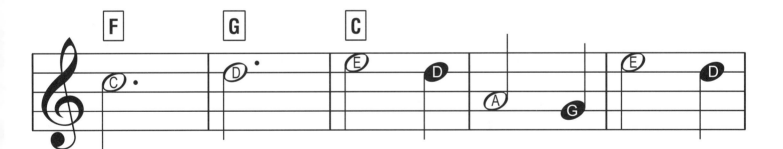

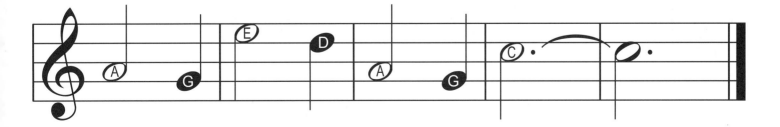

# Aria Math
## from MINECRAFT: VOLUME BETA

Registration 5
Rhythm: 16-Beat or Calypso

By Daniel Rosenfeld

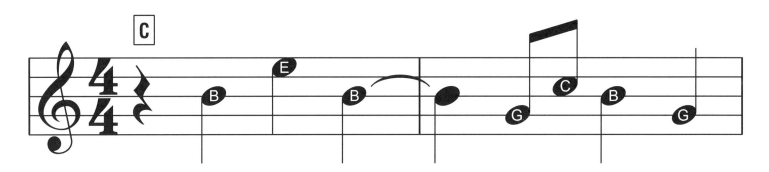

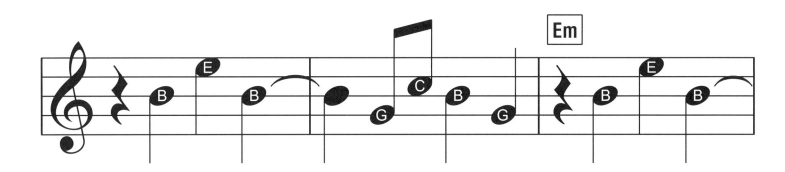

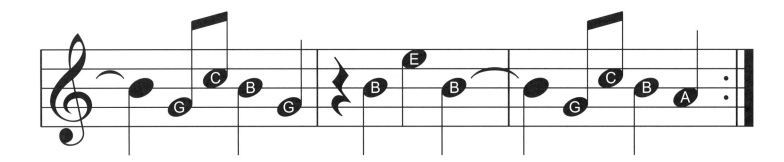

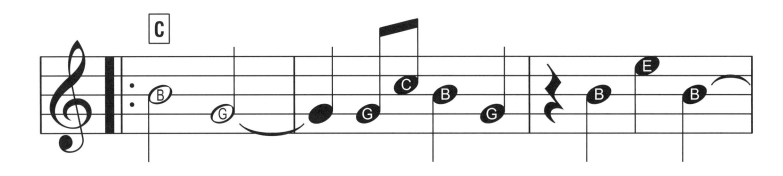

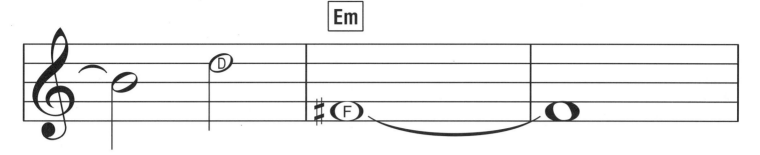
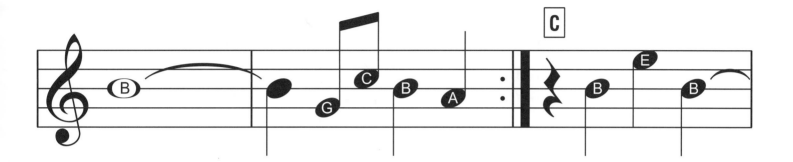
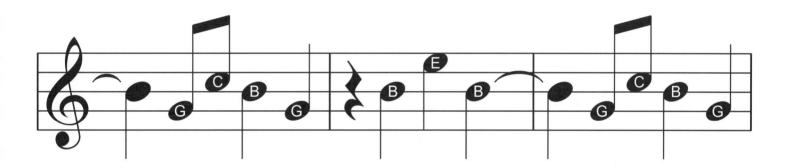
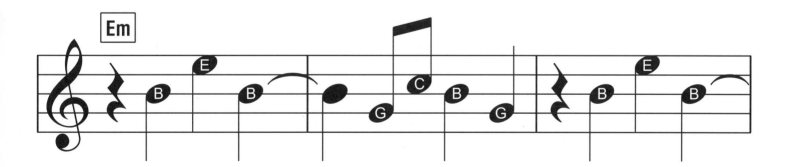
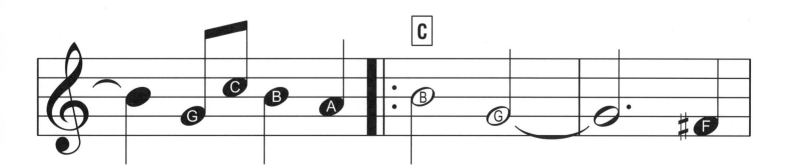

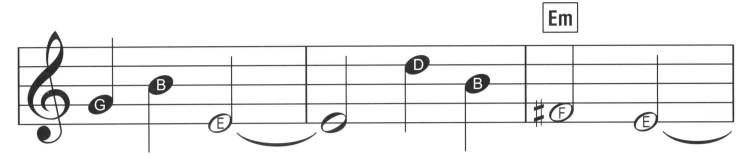

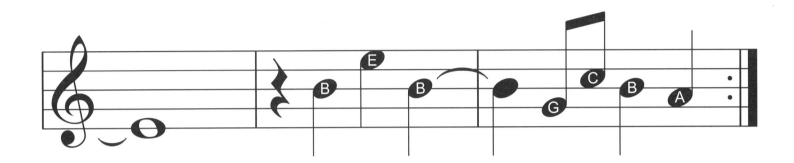

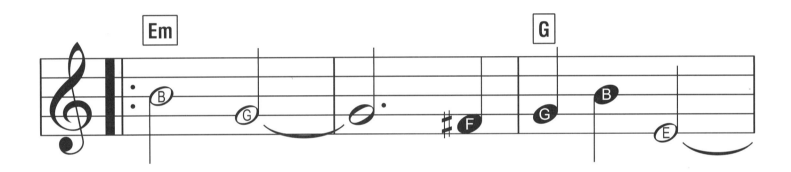

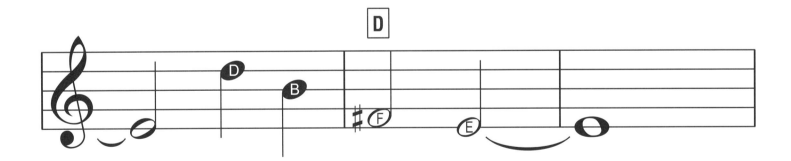

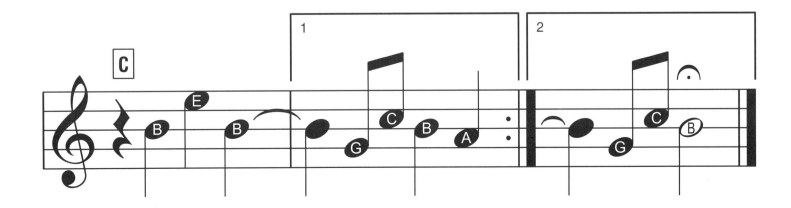

# Cat
## from MINECRAFT: VOLUME ALPHA

Registration 9
Rhythm: 8-Beat or Pop

By Daniel Rosenfeld

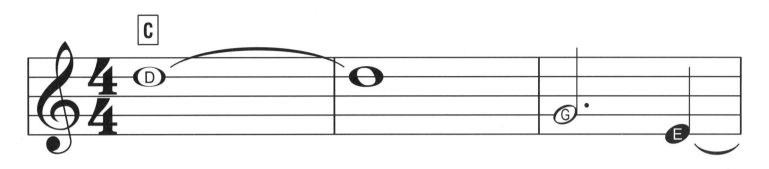

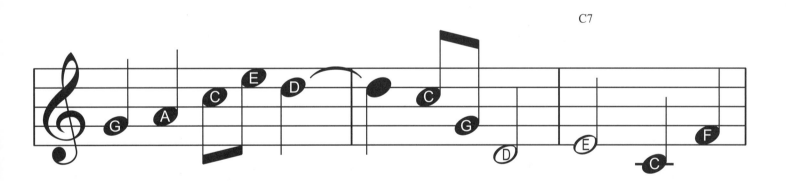

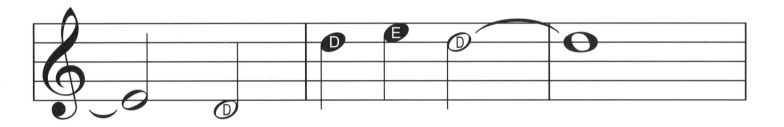

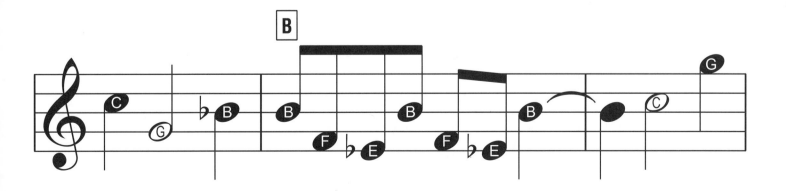

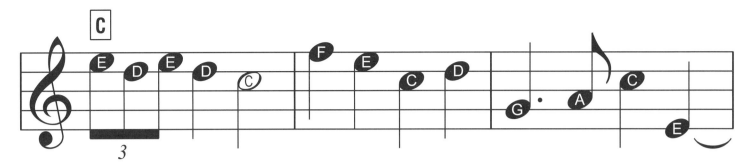

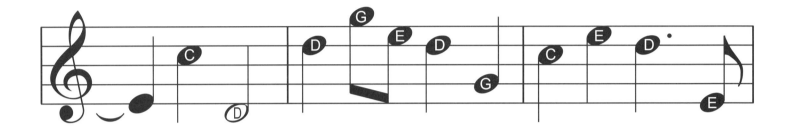

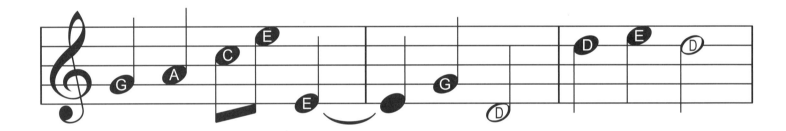

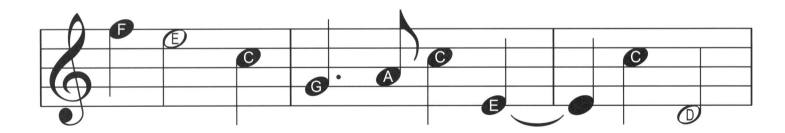

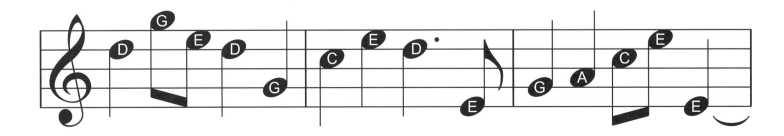

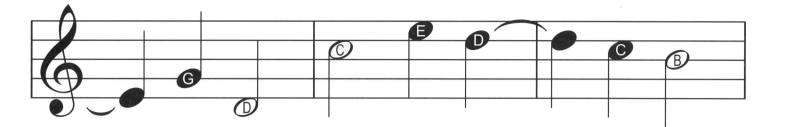

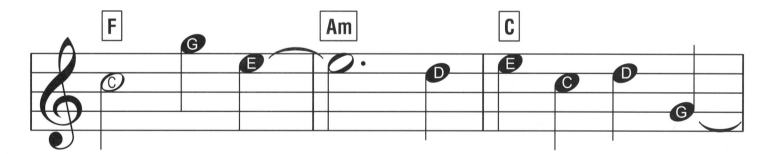

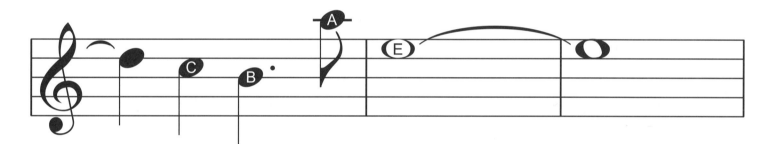

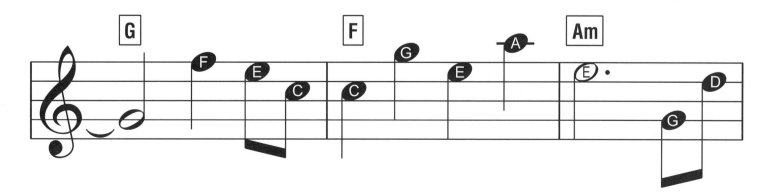

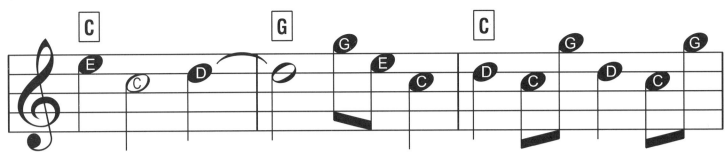

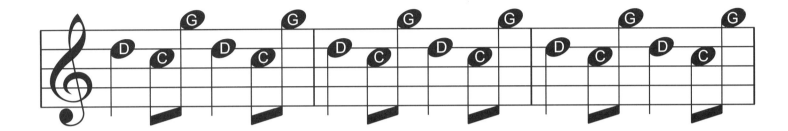

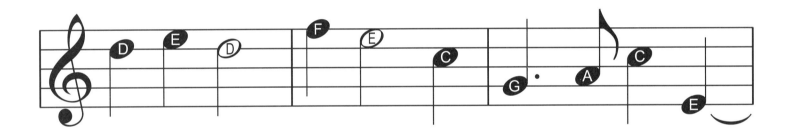

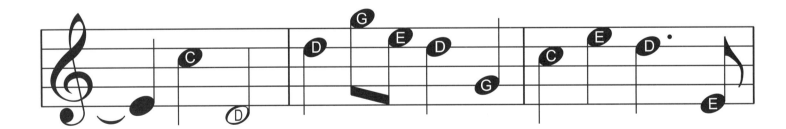

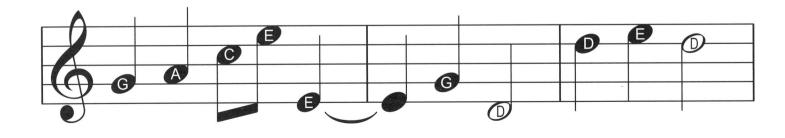

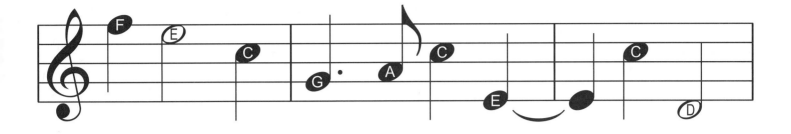

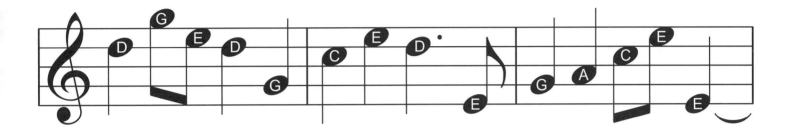

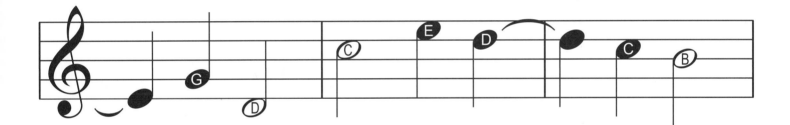

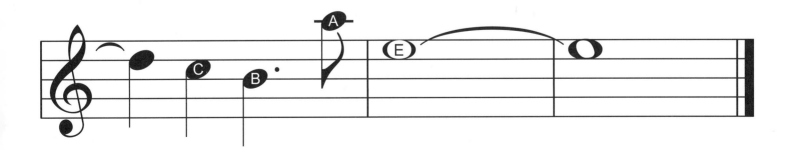

# Door
## from MINECRAFT: VOLUME ALPHA

Registration 8
Rhythm: Ballad or None

By Daniel Rosenfeld

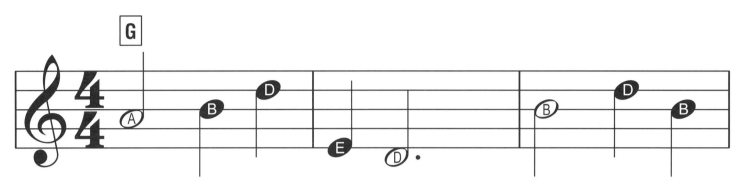

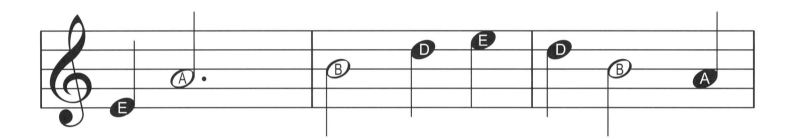

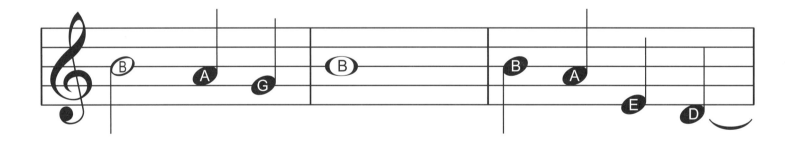

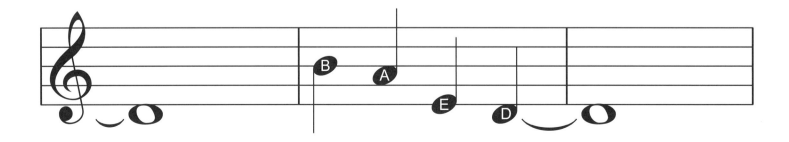

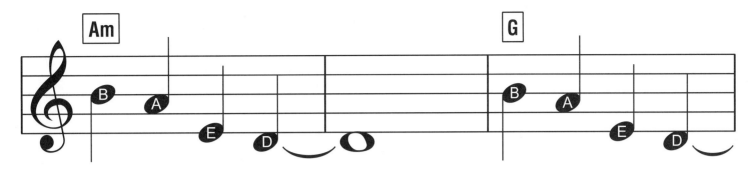

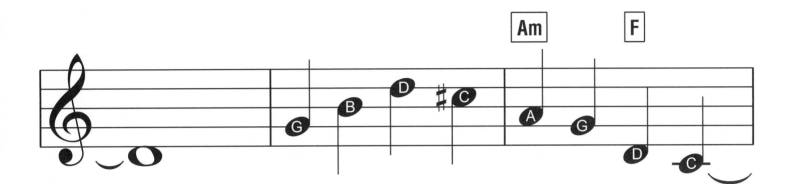

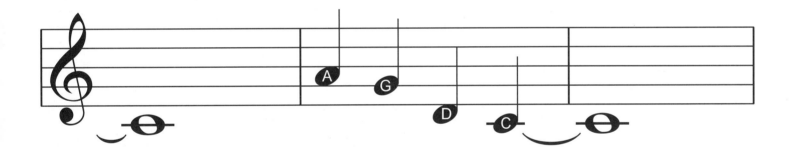

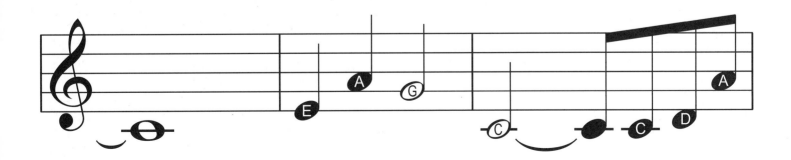

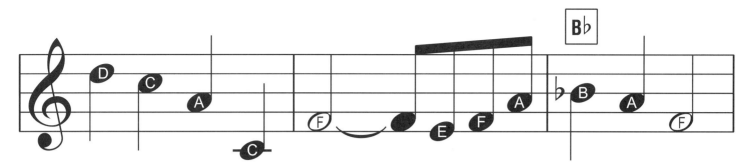

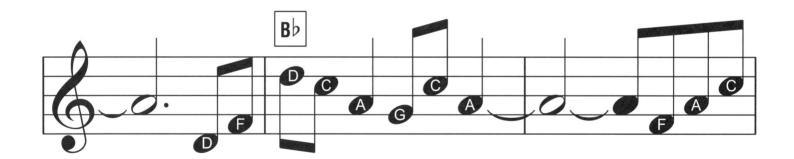

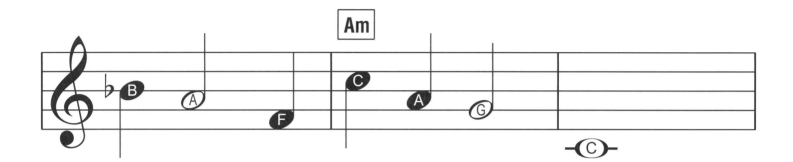

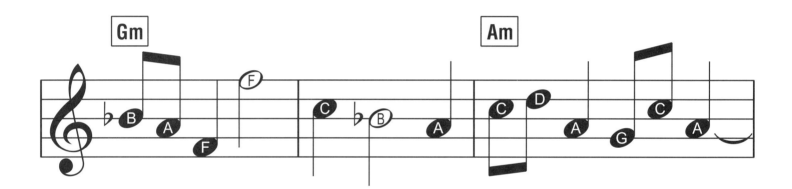

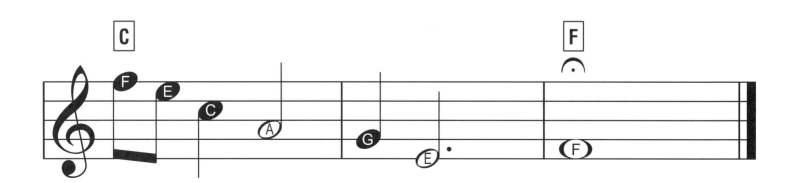

# Living Mice
## from MINECRAFT: VOLUME ALPHA

By Daniel Rosenfeld

Registration 8
Rhythm: Ballad

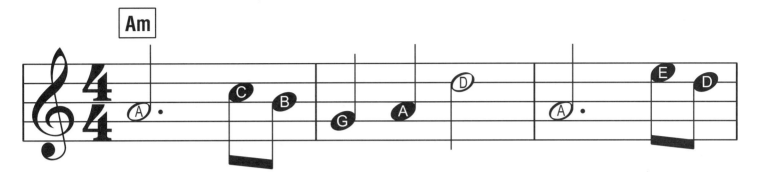

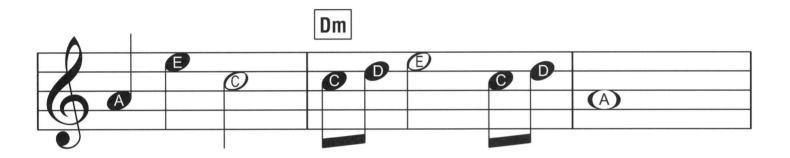

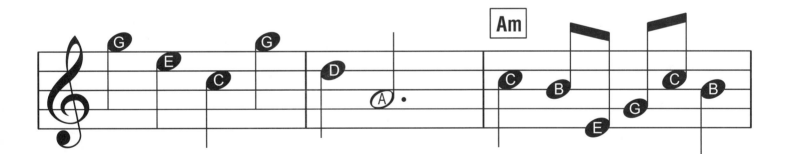

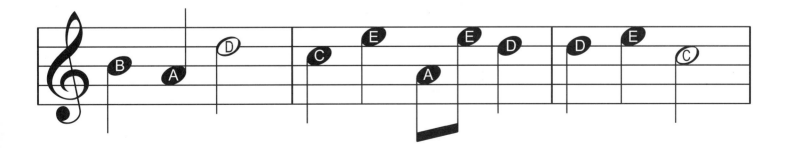

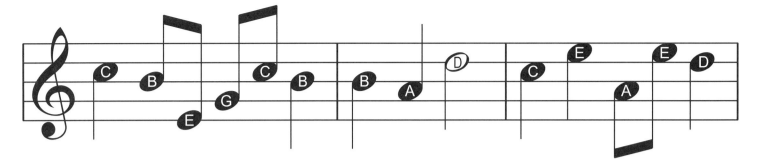

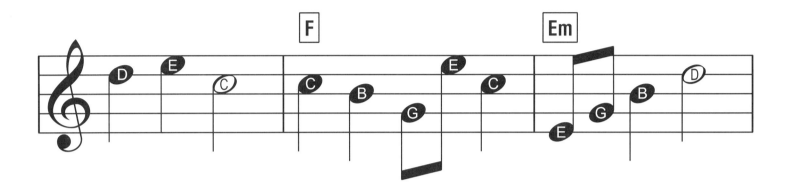

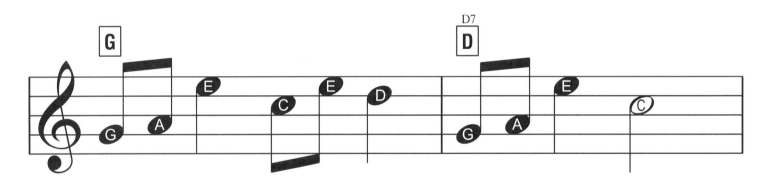

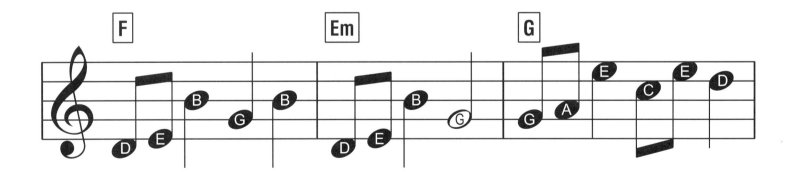

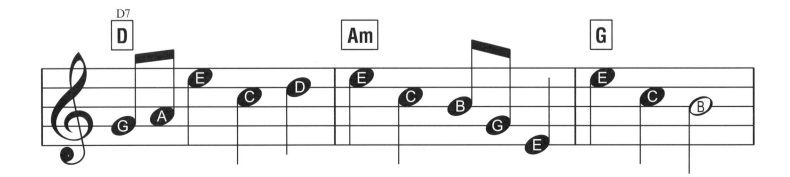

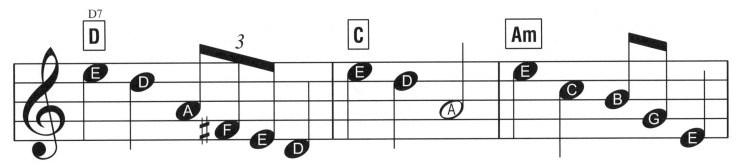

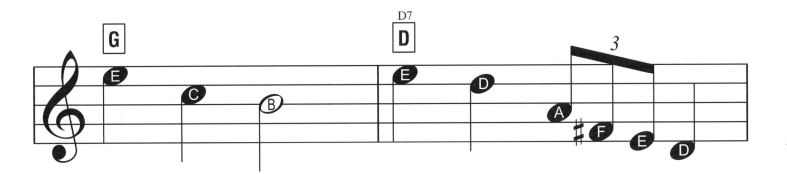

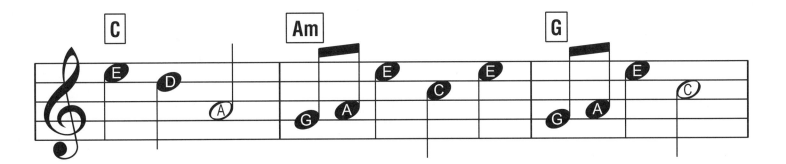

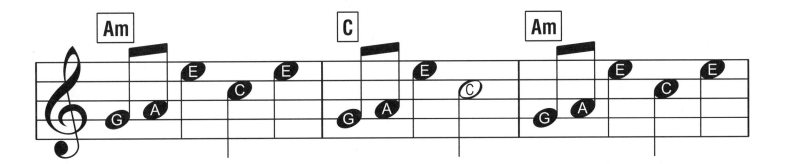

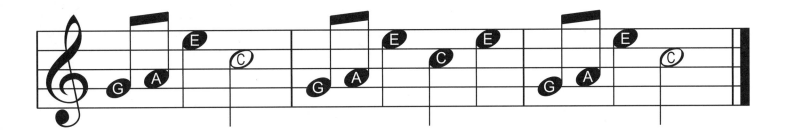

# Mice on Venus
## from MINECRAFT: VOLUME ALPHA

Registration 8
Rhythm: Ballad or None

By Daniel Rosenfeld

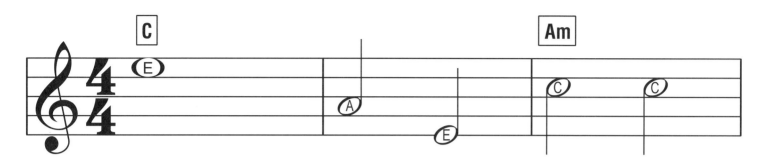

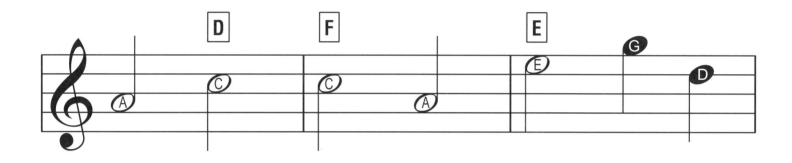

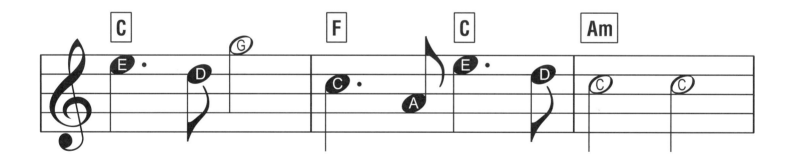

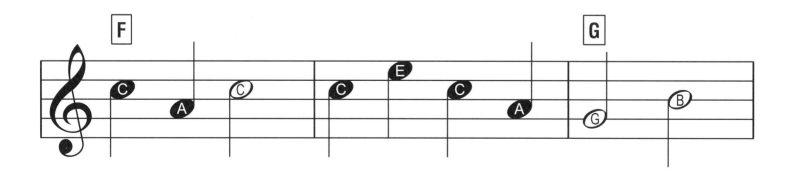

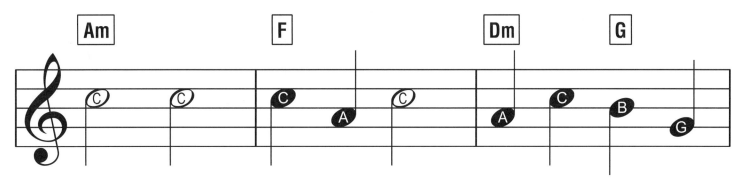

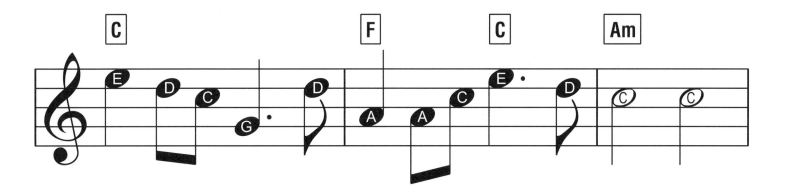

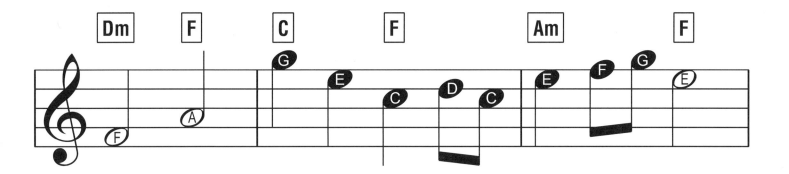

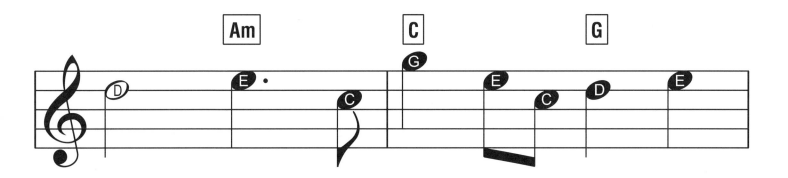

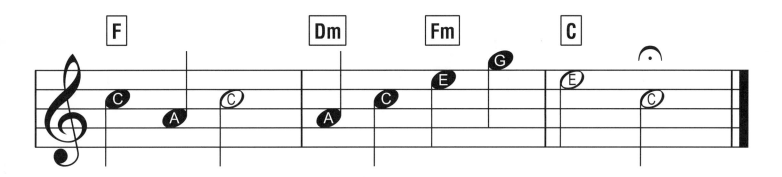

# Minecraft
## from MINECRAFT: VOLUME ALPHA

Registration 8
Rhythm: Ballad or None

By Daniel Rosenfeld

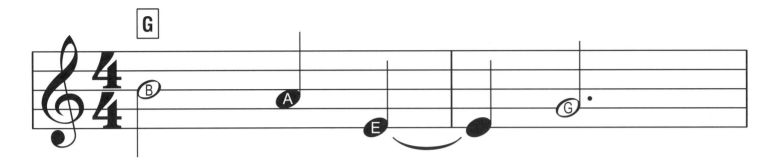

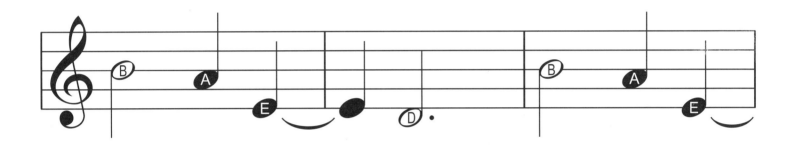

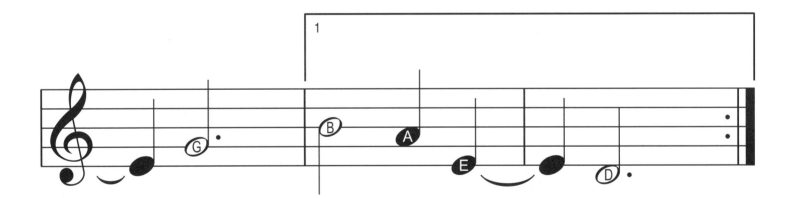

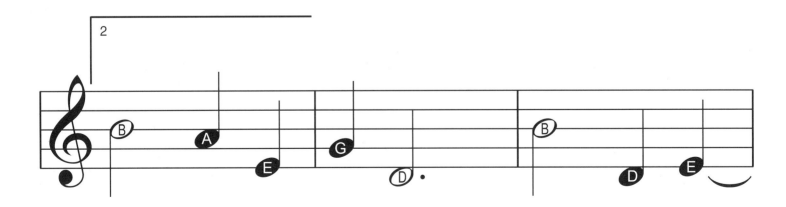

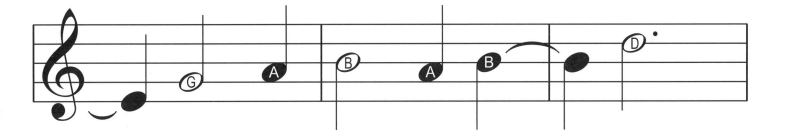

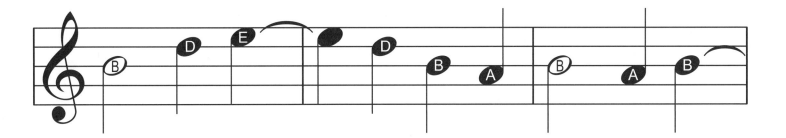

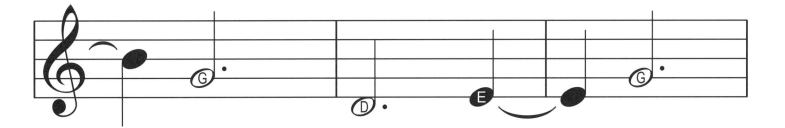

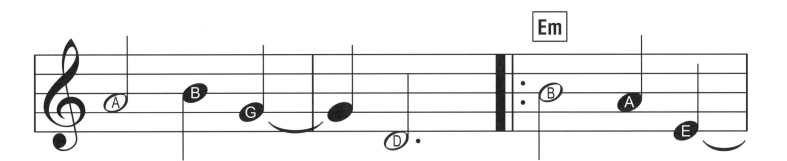

**Play 4 times**

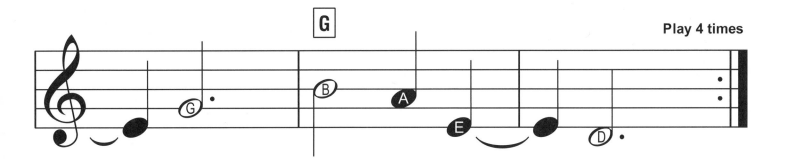

# Mutation
## from MINECRAFT: VOLUME BETA

Registration 8
Rhythm: Ballad or None

By Daniel Rosenfeld

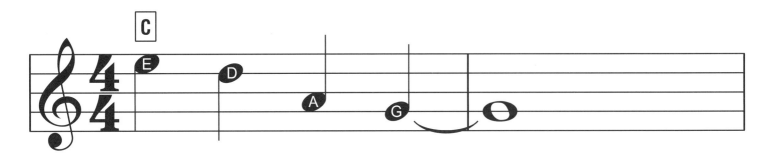

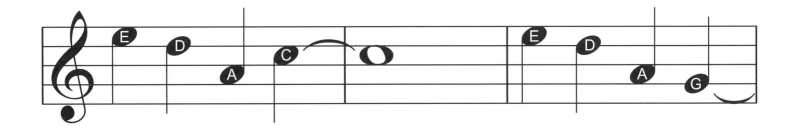

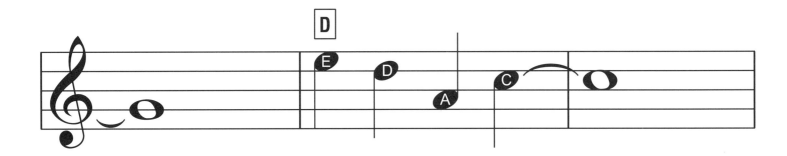

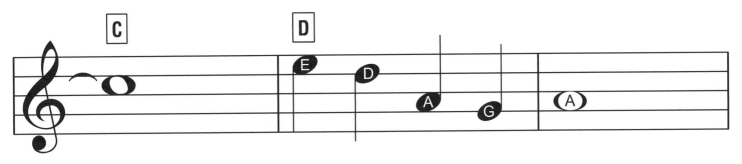

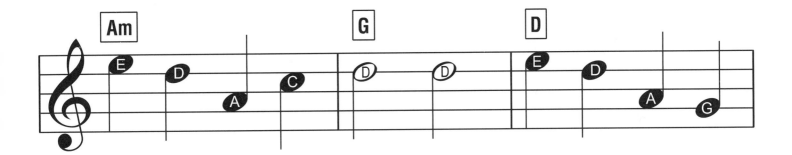

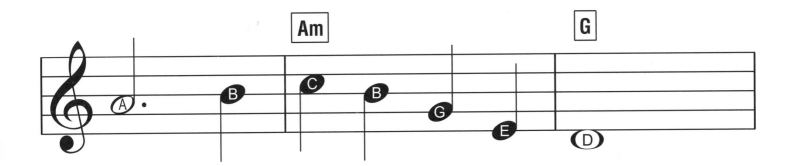

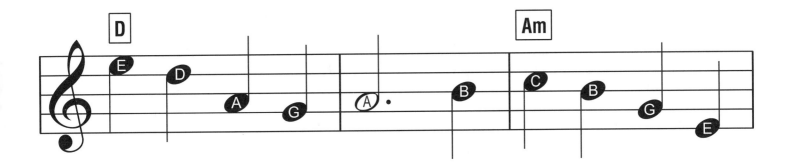

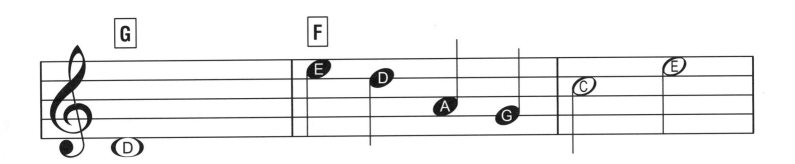

27

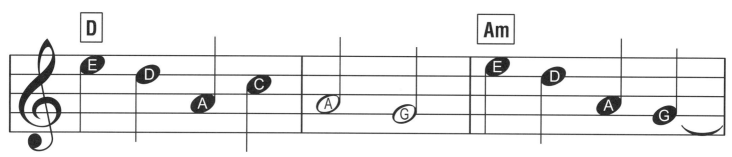

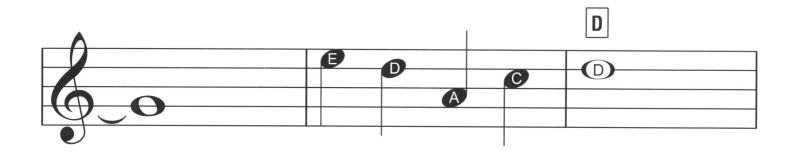

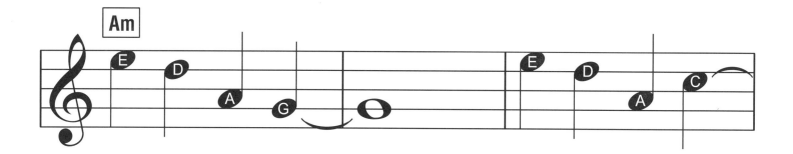

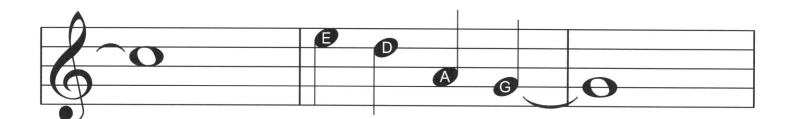

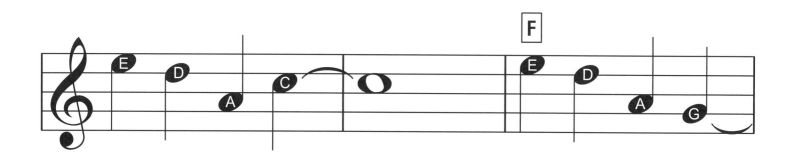

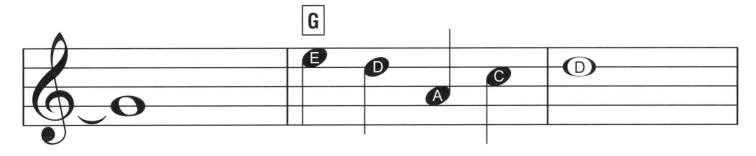

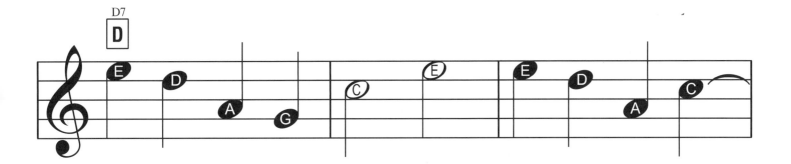

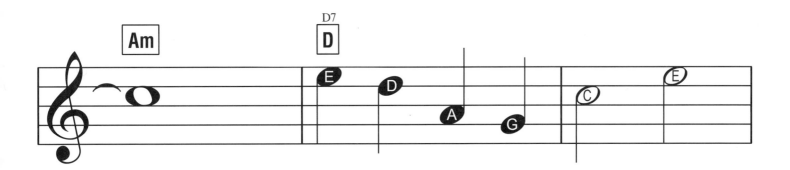

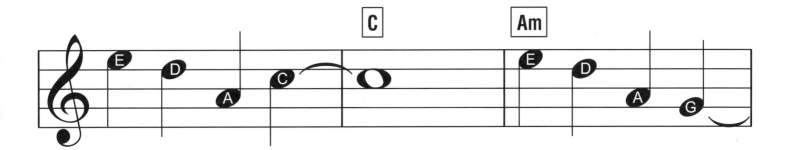

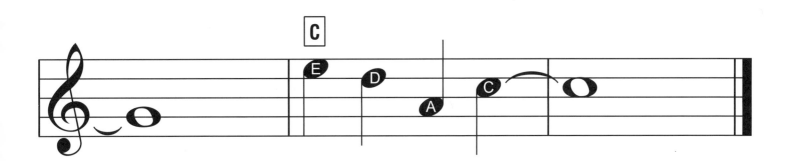

# Subwoofer Lullaby
## from MINECRAFT: VOLUME ALPHA

Registration 8
Rhythm: Ballad or 8-Beat

By Daniel Rosenfeld

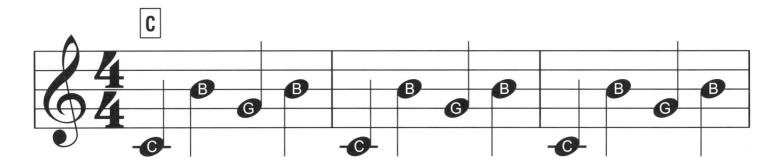

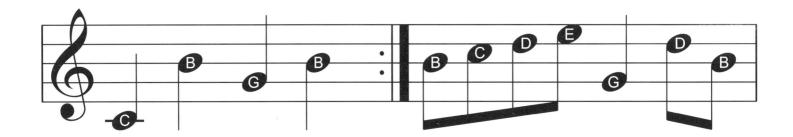

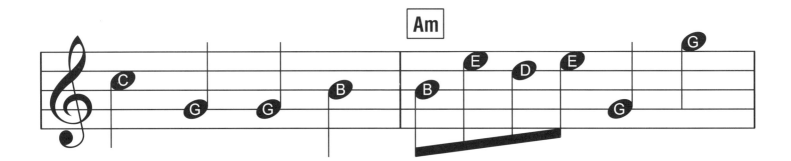

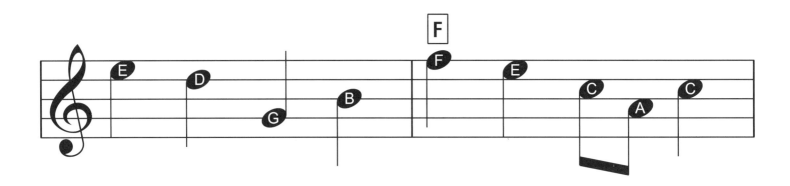

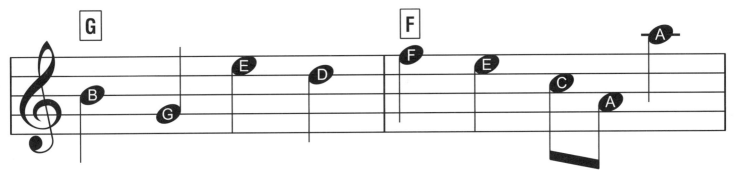

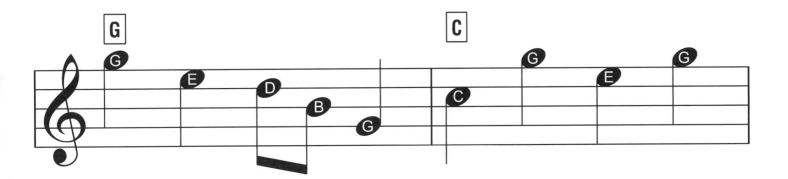

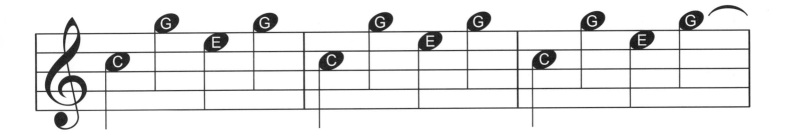

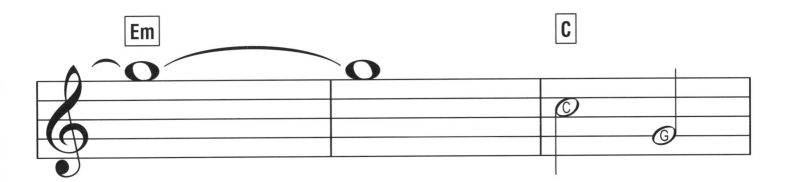

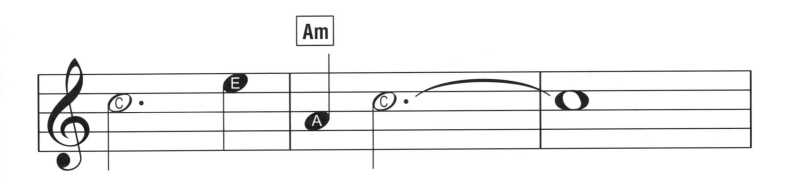

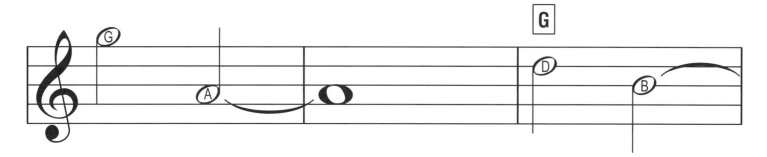

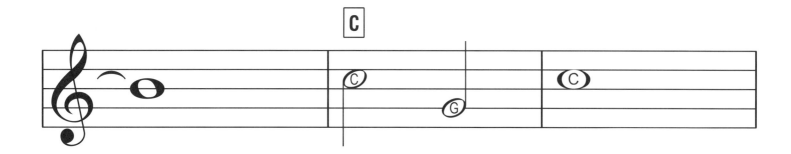

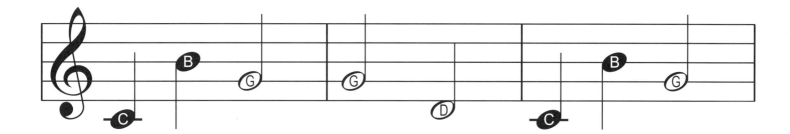

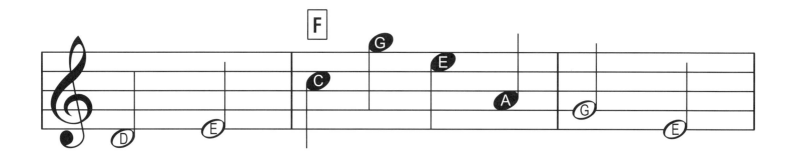

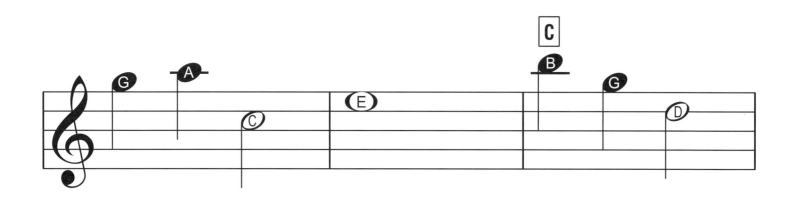

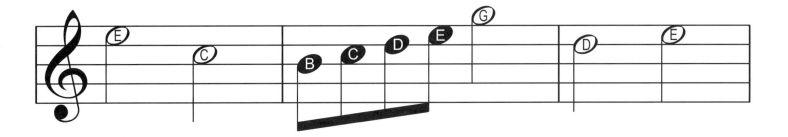

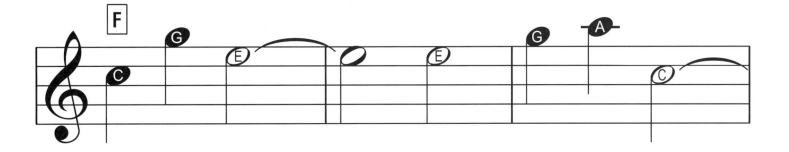

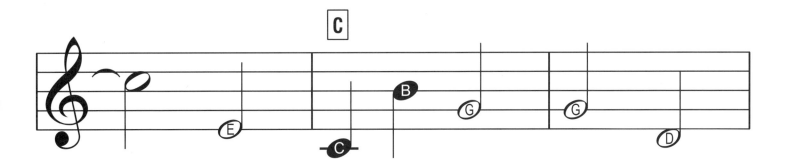

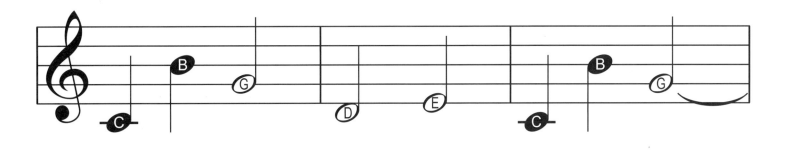

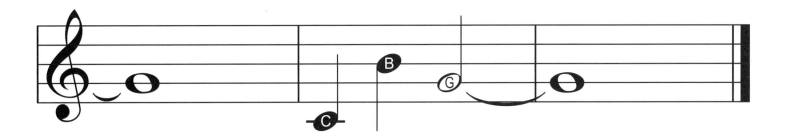

# Sweden
## from MINECRAFT: VOLUME ALPHA

Registration 8
Rhythm: Ballad or None

By Daniel Rosenfeld

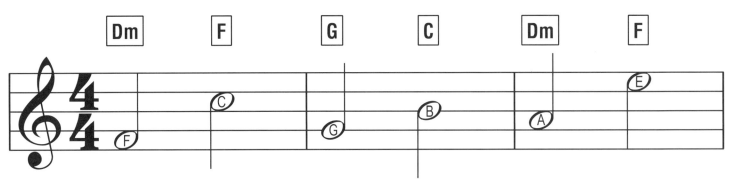

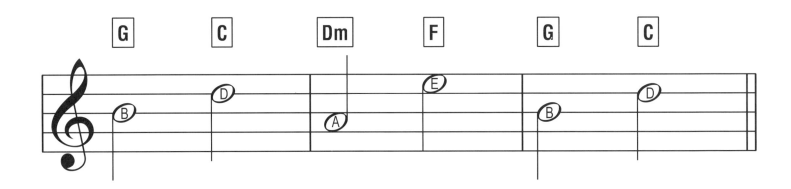

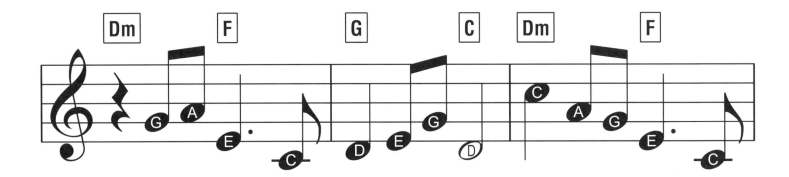

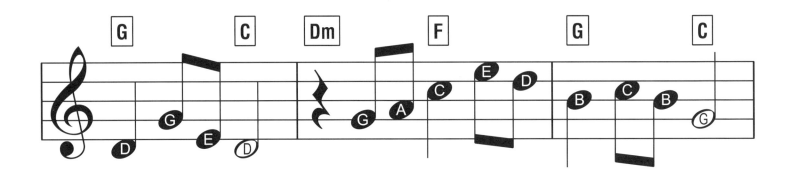

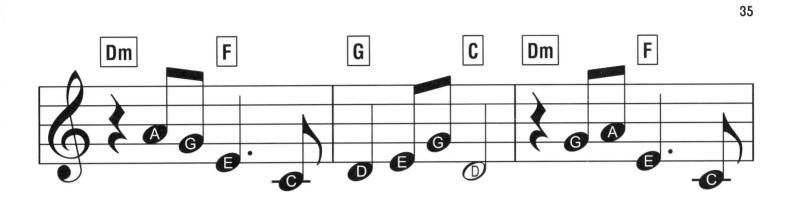

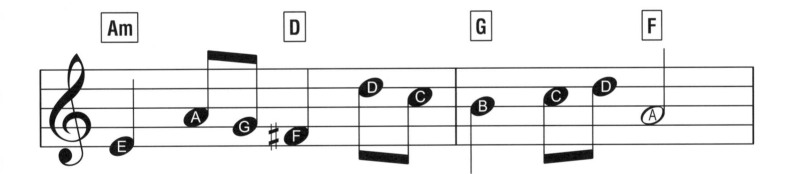

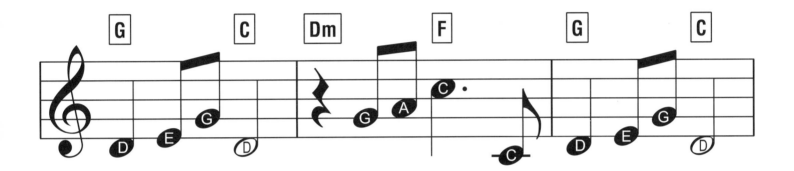

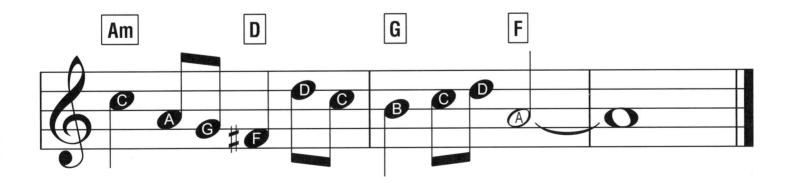

# Wet Hands
## from MINECRAFT: VOLUME ALPHA

Registration 8
Rhythm: Ballad

By Daniel Rosenfeld

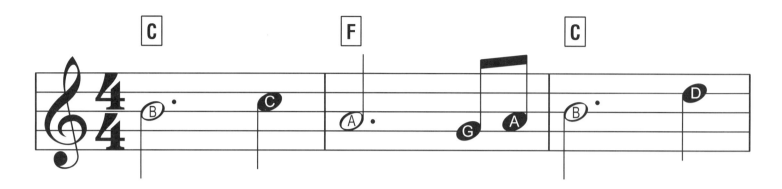

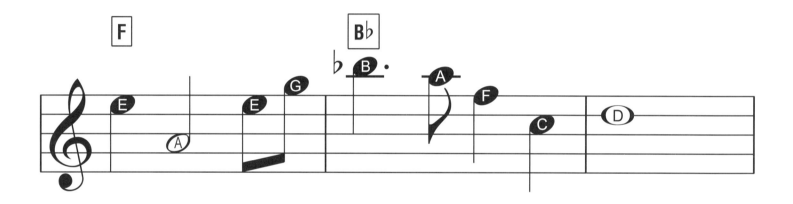

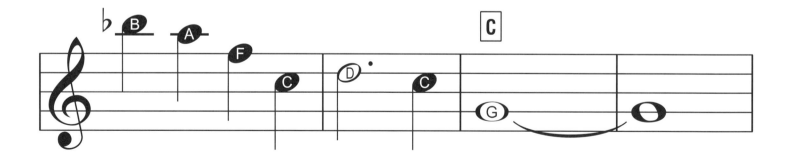

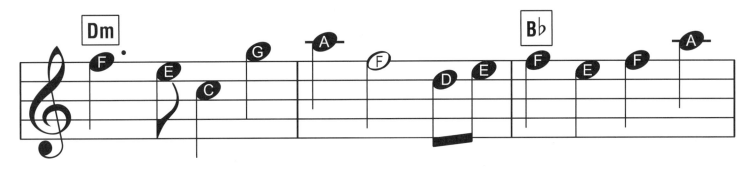

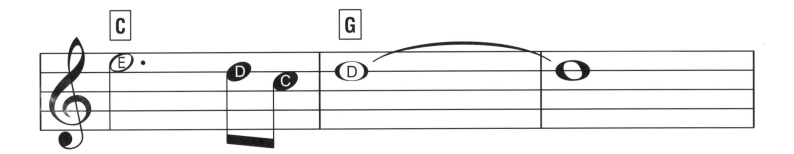

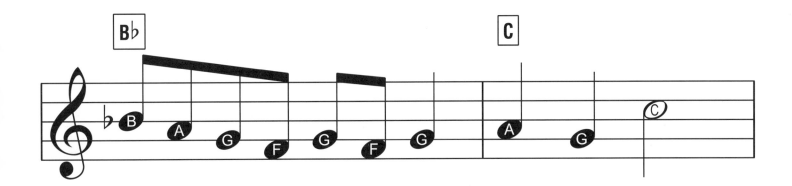

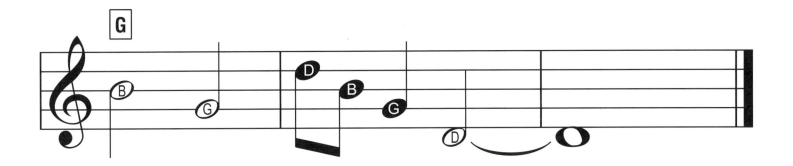

# Moog City
## from MINECRAFT: VOLUME ALPHA

Registration 7
Rhythm: 8-Beat

By Daniel Rosenfeld

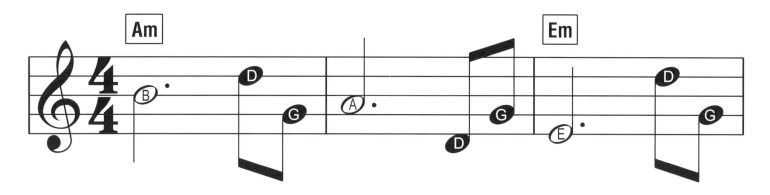

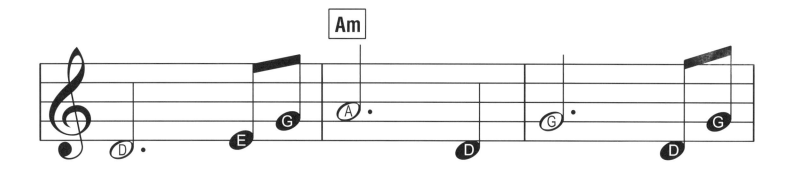

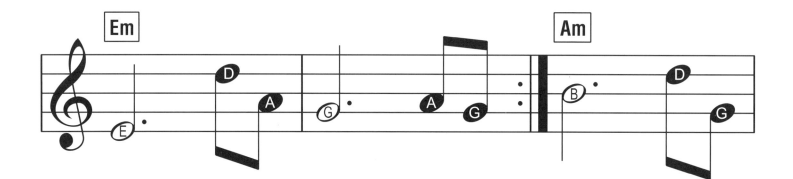

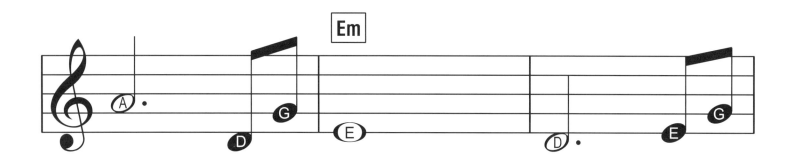

39

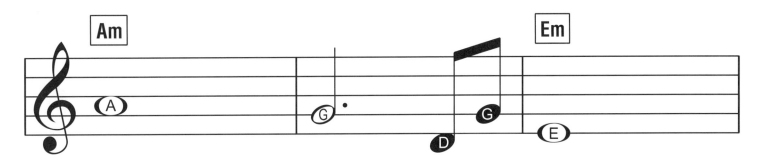

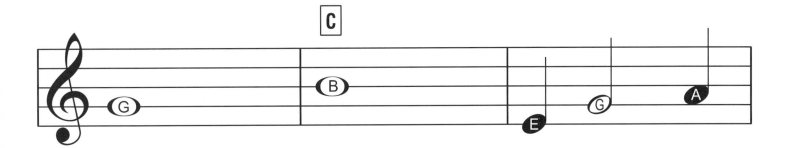

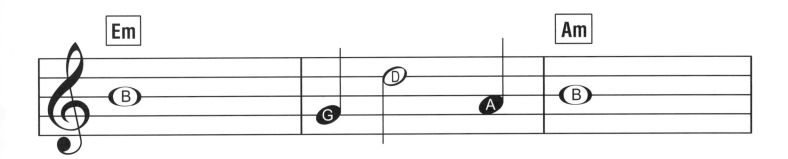

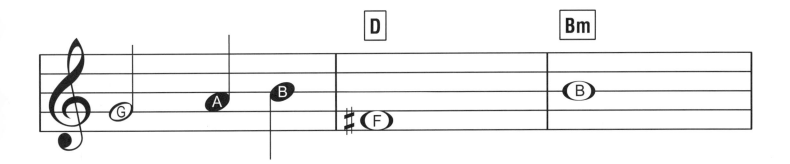

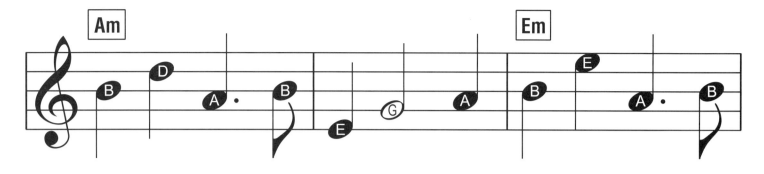

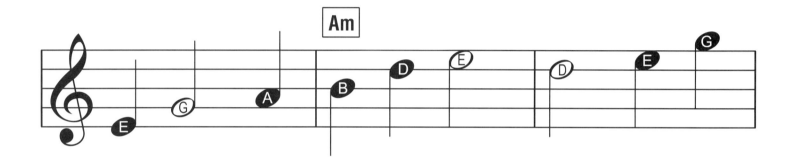

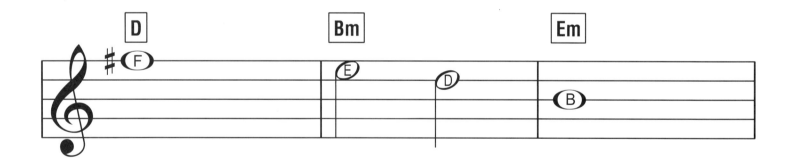

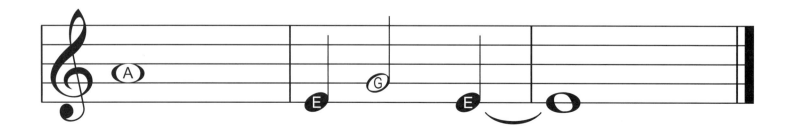